W9-AJP-893

ALABAMA

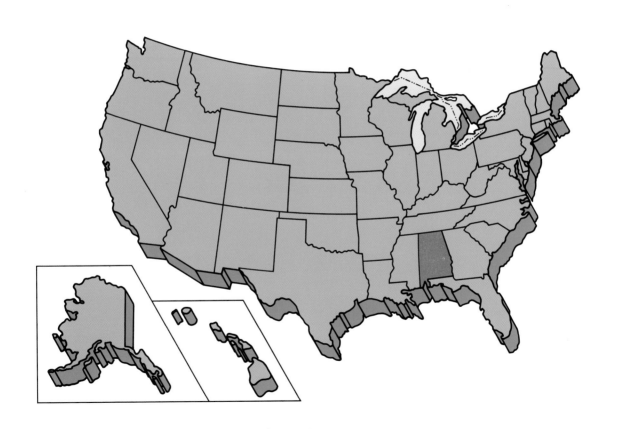

Hello U.S.A.

ALABAMA

Dottie Brown

Lerner Publications Company

Cover photograph by Johnny Autery.

The glossary on page 69 gives definitions of words shown in **bold type** in the text.

LIBRARY OF CONGRESS
CATALOGING-IN-PUBLICATION DATA
Brown, Dottie.
    Alabama / by Dottie Brown.
      p. cm. — (Hello USA)
    Includes index.
    ISBN 0-8225-2741-3 (lib. bdg.)
    1. Alabama—Juvenile literature. [1. Alabama.]
I. Title. II. Series.
F326.3.B76 1994
976.1—dc20
                              93-37796
                                 CIP
                                 AC

Manufactured in the United States of America

1 2 3 4 5 6 – I/JR – 99 98 97 96 95 94

 This book is printed on acid-free, recyclable paper.

CONTENTS

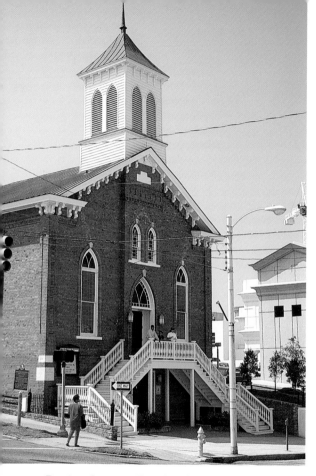

Dexter Avenue Baptist Church

6

Did You Know . . . ?

❑ Scientists at the Marshall Space Flight Center in Huntsville, Alabama, developed the spacecraft that thrust U.S. astronauts all the way to the moon.

❑ Alabama takes its name from the Alibamu, an Indian group that once lived in the region. Alibamu means "I clear the thicket."

❑ In 1955 Martin Luther King, Jr., a minister, started the black **civil rights movement** at the Dexter Avenue Baptist Church in Montgomery, Alabama. King's nonviolent protests led to fairer treatment for African Americans.

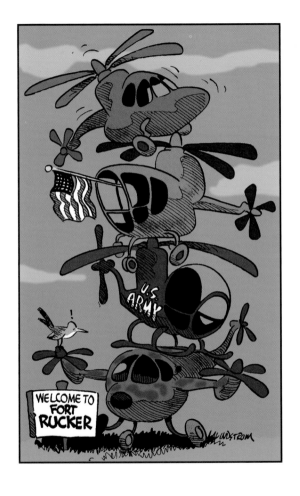

❑ The U.S. Army Aviation Museum at Fort Rucker in Alabama houses more than 100 helicopters, making it one of the largest collections of choppers in the nation.

❑ Alabama almost split into two states. Just before the Civil War began in 1861, northern Alabamians came close to forming a new state called Nick-a-Jack. The founders of Nick-a-Jack did not want to withdraw from the United States, as Alabama had done.

❑ During the Civil War, Montgomery became the first capital of the Confederacy, or union of Southern states. For this reason, Montgomery is still called the Cradle of the Confederacy.

A Trip Around the State

Dixie is a word used to describe the South, a region that covers the southeastern section of the United States. Alabama, located near the center of this region, is known as the Heart of Dixie.

The Dixie state of Alabama is bordered by four other southern states—Mississippi, Georgia, Tennessee, and Florida. The Gulf of Mexico, part of the Atlantic Ocean, washes against the southwestern tip of Alabama.

Rivers flow throughout much of Alabama. The state's longest rivers are the Alabama and the Tombigbee. These waterways meet in southwestern Alabama and form the Mobile River, which flows through Mobile Bay into the Gulf. Other chief rivers include the Tennessee and the Chattahoochee.

Locks—or water-filled chambers that allow boats to pass waterfalls—have been built along some of Alabama's rivers. Huge dams on these waterways control water depth to help prevent flooding. The dams hold back extra water after heavy rains, forming **reservoirs**, or artificial lakes. The lake water is then slowly released to power engines that produce electricity.

The reservoirs also supply water to nearby cities and towns. Alabama's largest lakes are actually reservoirs. The biggest are Guntersville, Wheeler, and Weiss.

Lakes and rivers are found in all of Alabama's three regions—the Appalachian Highlands, the Gulf

Water from a reservoir rushes through gates at the Millers Ferry dam on the Alabama River. The force of the flowing water powers nearby engines, which generate electricity.

Coastal Plain, and the Black Belt. The landscapes of these regions vary from flat, sandy beaches to low, pine-covered mountains.

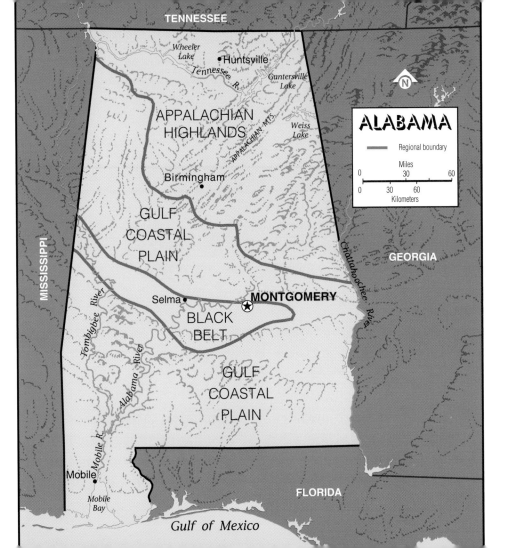

11

The highest point in Alabama is Cheaha, in the Appalachian Highlands. The mountain peak rises 2,407 feet (734 meters).

The Appalachian Highlands region is situated in the northeastern part of the state. This area contains the southern end of the Appalachian Mountains, the oldest mountain system in North America. Minerals such as coal, iron ore, and limestone lie beneath many of the highlands' ridges and valleys. Birmingham, Alabama's largest city, sits on top of some of these deposits.

Alabama's largest land region, the Gulf Coastal Plain, covers nearly two-thirds of the state. Low, rolling hills cover the northern half of the plain. **Swamps,** or wetlands, fill the flat southwestern section of the region. Soil along much of the western edge of the plain is too rocky and sandy to farm, but the rich soil in the eastern area is suitable for many crops.

The Black Belt is a strip of gently rolling land that slices through the middle of the Gulf Coastal Plain. The fertile black soil of the belt is some of Alabama's best farmland. At one time, cotton **plantations,** or large farms, sprawled across the region. Nowadays, many farmers raise livestock and grow vegetables in the Black Belt.

Dauphin Island, part of Alabama's Gulf Coastal Plain, lies in the Gulf of Mexico.

Lightning strikes a tree during a storm in western Alabama.

A long growing season benefits Alabama's farmers. The state's weather is generally mild in the winter and hot in the summer. During the winter, northern Alabama is slightly colder than the southern half of the state. The average winter temperature throughout Alabama is a warm 50°F (10°C). Summer temperatures tend to be about the same all over the state, averaging around 80°F (27°C).

Alabama is a well-watered land. An average of 59 inches (150 centimeters) of **precipitation** (rain and melted snow) fall each year in the state, mostly as rain. Northern Alabama gets a few light snowfalls in winter.

Tornadoes and hurricanes occasionally blast through the state. These fierce storms can yank up trees, rip apart homes, and mangle docks. Most of the time, however, Alabama's weather is tame.

Torn from the ground during a severe storm, a large oak tree lies rootless.

During the spring, a field of wildflowers hides part of a fence.

Forests of pine, cedar, cypress, hemlock, and oak blanket about two-thirds of Alabama. Spanish moss, a plant that grows without roots, drapes itself over tree limbs. Many fragrant, flowering trees and shrubs such as magnolias, dogwoods, mountain laurels, and azaleas perfume the air. Orchids, asters, goldenrods, and other flowering plants add their beauty to the forests.

Wooded areas are home to much of Alabama's wildlife, too. Bobcats stalk rabbits in the state's tree-covered mountains. Red foxes and gray foxes prowl through dense stands of trees, where opossums, mink, and skunks scurry about. Alligators slither through Alabama's southern swamps, and beavers gnaw saplings, which the animals use to build their homes in the state's lowlands.

Cottontail rabbit

Alligator

Spanish moss *(above)*
Cardinal flower *(inset)*

17

Alabama's Story

The glow of a blazing fire cast dancing shadows inside a huge cave in what is now northeastern Alabama. It was a chilly winter evening, and the hunters in the cave warmed themselves around the fire while supper roasted. An artist among them whiled away the time by painting pictures on the walls.

People who later found these paintings realized that the cave's inhabitants weren't just ordinary campers. Scientists examined the hunting and cooking tools left behind and determined that the hunters most likely lived about 8,000 years ago. They were probably Alabama's first people.

Traces of other early peoples exist throughout the state. Burial mounds heaped up about 800 years ago by Indians known as mound builders still stand in southeastern Alabama. The mound-building Indians lived in villages and planted corn. They traveled far to trade pottery and jewelry for copper and seashells with other Indians.

At Mound State Monument in Moundville, Alabama, lie burial mounds *(facing page)* built by Native Americans *(inset, facing page)* hundreds of years ago.

19

Some experts believe that mound builders are the ancestors of the Choctaw, Chickasaw, and Creek Indians. Members of these Native American nations hunted and fished in Alabama. They were also good farmers who grew corn, beans, squash, and melons. The Indians of these nations shared some customs and spoke a similar language, called Muskogean.

Indians were living in Alabama for hundreds of years before Spanish explorer Hernando de Soto arrived in 1540. De Soto, the first European to explore the region, marched a band of 950 soldiers into Choctaw territory to look for gold. A group of Choctaw Indians, who considered the armed Spaniards to be intruders, barred their way. But the Spaniards broke through, killed the Indians, and burned their village.

A few other Spaniards visited the region after de Soto, but the French were the first to establish a permanent European settlement there. In 1702, two French Canadian brothers, Pierre and

Hernando de Soto

From 1702 until 1722, Fort Louis de la Mobile served as capital of the Louisiana Territory. This large stretch of land was claimed by France in 1682.

Jean Baptiste Le Moyne, founded Fort Louis de la Mobile on a bluff near the Mobile River.

Because of flooding, the fort was moved farther south in 1711 to what is now the city of Mobile, and in 1720 the fort was renamed Fort Condé. In 1763, at the end of the French and Indian War, the French lost Fort Condé and most of their other North American holdings to the British and the Spanish. As a result, Britain claimed almost all the land between the Mississippi River and the Atlantic Ocean, including Alabama.

21

Along the Atlantic coast, Britain had divided its territory into **colonies**. In 1775, to gain their independence, 13 of the colonies started fighting Britain in a war that became known as the American Revolution. Britain lost the war in 1783, and the 13 former colonies formed a new country—the United States of America.

But Britain had lost more than the colonies. It also had to give much of its land in North America to Spain, which had assisted the colonists in battle. Spain then agreed to give some territory, including most of what is now Alabama, to the United States.

People from the States began moving into Alabama looking for fertile farmland. Many newcomers settled on the Indians' territory. Besides the Choctaw, Chickasaw, and Creek, the Cherokee Indians now lived in Alabama. These nations tried to get along with the settlers, adopting European customs. But they could not allow the newcomers to keep taking Indian land.

Some settlers grew tobacco on Alabama's abundant farmland.

Tecumseh Puts His Foot Down

Tecumseh, a Shawnee Indian leader who was living in Detroit, Michigan, traveled across the country working to unite all Indians against white settlers. In 1811 he reached the Creek village of Tuckabatchee in Alabama. Indians there refused to join Tecumseh in his plans for war, which angered the leader. According to one story, Tecumseh said, "When I get back to Detroit, I will stamp my foot upon the ground and shake every house in Tuckabatchee."

One month later—about the time Tecumseh reached Detroit—a powerful earthquake shook parts of Alabama. The Indians of Tuckabatchee ran from their homes shouting, "Tecumseh has reached Detroit! We feel the shake of his foot!"

In 1813, angry about losing their land, a group of Indians known as the Red Stick Creek attacked Fort Mims, a pioneer settlement on the Alabama River. The Indians killed hundreds of men, women, and children.

Another band of Creek called the White Stick joined the Chickasaw, Choctaw, and Cherokee Indians against the Red Stick Creek in what became known as the Creek War. In 1814 these Indians, along with U.S. troops led by General

Pioneers at Fort Mims were caught by surprise when Creek Indians attacked in 1813. In this painting, the artist pictured the pioneers as helpless.

Andrew Jackson, won the Battle of Horseshoe Bend. Afterward, the general insisted that all Creek—including the White Stick—give up their land, which covered about half of present-day Alabama. The Creek had to move to a small area in eastern Alabama.

The war opened up land to U.S. settlers, who began to pour into Alabama. They came from Virginia, Georgia, Tennessee, and beyond. Some of Alabama's new settlers were blacksmiths, machinists, and wagon makers who had come to fight in the Creek War and decided to stay. All were looking for a better life in a fertile land. By 1819 Alabama had a large enough population to become the 22nd state of the United States.

Since becoming a state in 1819, Alabama has changed its flag several times. The above design, which is still in use, dates to 1895. It is modeled after the Confederate flag used during the Civil War.

Most Alabamians owned small plots of land, which they farmed themselves. But some planters used black people, who had been forced to come to America from Africa, to work cotton plantations. These slave-owning planters earned the most money for Alabama. Cotton, which was grown mainly to make clothing, was so important to the state's economy that the fluffy white crop was called King Cotton.

The planters grew their cotton in the fertile soil of Alabama's Black Belt. The dirt was rich in the nutrients needed to grow healthy crops, but the land was hard to plow. Planters depended on slaves to do the difficult jobs of plowing

the fields and handpicking the cotton at harvesttime.

Montgomery, on the edge of the Black Belt, was the town where buyers and sellers of cotton bargained for the best prices. It became the center of activity—a prosperous town where doctors, lawyers, merchants, and bankers built elegant mansions.

Slaves *(foreground)* **worked hard to produce crops that were sold in Montgomery** *(background),* **an agricultural center of the South since the 1800s.**

By the mid-1800s, about one-third of Alabamians owned slaves, and nearly everyone in the state depended in one way or another on plantations worked by slaves. Some purchased the cotton from planters and then sold it to clothing manufacturers for a profit. Others simply wore the clothing made from Alabama's cotton.

While the South relied on slave labor, the North, with its factories and smaller farms, did not. Many Northerners believed slavery was wrong and tried to persuade the U.S. government to make slavery illegal in all states.

Southern plantation owners argued that they would go broke if they had to give up slaves. Southerners also believed strongly in the right to make their own decisions and disliked Northerners meddling in Southern affairs.

Planters welcomed the cotton gin. This invention saved time and money by removing seeds from cotton much faster than people could.

At a convention in Montgomery in 1861, Southern leaders named Jefferson Davis president of the Confederate States of America.

Abraham Lincoln, a Northerner, was elected president of the United States in 1860. Fearing that slavery would become illegal across the country, Alabama withdrew from the United States early in 1861. Several other Southern states joined Alabama and organized the Confederate States of America, a new country where slavery was legal. Shortly afterward the Civil War broke out between the North (the Union) and the South (the Confederacy).

At least 120,000 Alabamians fought for the Confederacy. The most important Civil War battle in Alabama took place at Mobile Bay in 1864. Union troops captured Mobile Bay and prevented the port from sending or receiving supplies.

The Union navy weakened Alabama by blocking its main port after the Battle of Mobile Bay.

The Union won the war in 1865, and all Confederate slaves were freed. After four long years of war, parts of Alabama were in shambles. Food and money were scarce. Union troops had looted and torched several towns, destroyed crops, and stolen livestock.

After the war, during a period known as **Reconstruction**, Northern lawmakers and businesspeople ran Alabama's government. They oversaw the building of new roads and made sure black people were given the right to vote. But many of the Northerners did more harm than good. Called **carpetbaggers** by Southerners, the dishonest and inexperienced Northerners stole or wasted government money, hurting the economy they were supposed to be helping.

A School of Their Own

After the Civil War, black Americans set out to carve a new place for themselves in society. They wanted to farm their own land and run their own businesses. Laws in the South prevented African Americans from attending white schools, so they opened schools of their own.

In 1881 a former slave named Booker T. Washington founded a school in Tuskegee, Alabama, for African Americans. Called the Tuskegee Normal and Industrial Institute, the school taught practical skills, giving black men and women a chance to find work and make money. Many graduates became farmers, teachers, and mechanics.

The school later changed its name to Tuskegee University and began offering bachelor's and master's degrees. Nowadays, the nearly 4,000 African American students at the university major in dozens of fields, including business, engineering, architecture, nursing, and veterinary medicine.

Much timber was needed to construct new buildings in Alabama and elsewhere in the South after the Civil War.

During Reconstruction, Alabamians set out to rebuild their state. Farmers readied the soil for planting cotton. With its rich supply of minerals, Birmingham began pro-

ducing large amounts of iron and steel. Workers laid railroad tracks so trains could carry the iron and steel to Northern markets. By the 1890s, cloth and lumber companies also had grown, providing jobs and money for the state.

The United States entered World War I in 1917, further boosting Alabama's economy. Shipbuilders in Mobile manufactured battleships, while farmers in the state grew food for soldiers. Workers at textile mills used Alabama's cotton to make military uniforms.

After the war, Alabama built highways and began making many new products, including copper wire, paper, tires, and freight cars. But people in the United States soon felt the effects of the Great Depression, a nationwide period of economic hardship that lasted throughout the 1930s. Banks and other businesses across the nation closed down. Many people lost their jobs and their savings.

The Great Depression forced many Alabama families into poverty.

Relief came when then President Franklin D. Roosevelt created thousands of new jobs nationwide through a program called the New Deal. For Alabama, one of the most important parts of the New Deal was the Tennessee Valley Authority (TVA), an organization formed in 1933. The TVA put hundreds of Alabamians to work building dams to control seasonal flooding on the Tennessee River and to generate electricity.

The electricity provided by the dams was inexpensive. Some companies moved to Alabama because cheap electric power would help keep business costs down. In addition, many homeowners in Alabama received electricity for the first time, allowing them to use modern conveniences such as lightbulbs and radios.

But the dams and reservoirs also permanently flooded acres and acres of land, forcing many people to abandon homes their families had owned for generations. Many of these Alabamians were against the TVA.

During World War II (1939–1945), TVA dams powered plants in northern Alabama where missiles, rockets, and other military equipment were produced. After the war, a team of scientists came to one of these plants, the Redstone Arsenal in Huntsville, and developed the nation's first earth satellite. The satellite gathered information about space and about the planet Earth.

Alabamians constructed the *Cayuse 269* for the U.S. Navy during World War II.

While technology advanced, African Americans throughout the country were held back. Many were denied jobs because of their color. Black people did not have the same rights as white people.

In Alabama and other southern states, laws called Jim Crow laws prevented blacks from using the same drinking fountains, hospitals, elevators, and cemeteries as whites.

Rosa Parks Says No to Jim Crow

On her way home from work one day in 1955, a woman named Rosa Parks, from Montgomery, sat on a seat in the middle of a city bus. After all the seats in the front of the bus were taken, the driver ordered Parks to give up her seat for another passenger and to move to the rear. Parks refused and was arrested.

Parks, an African American, was asked to move so a white person could have her seat. One Jim Crow law enforced throughout the South stated that black people had to sit at the back of buses.

Rosa Parks's arrest outraged a young black minister in Montgomery, Martin Luther King, Jr., and he immediately organized a peaceful protest. African Americans refused to ride the city's buses for more than a year. The protest ended in 1956 when the U.S. Supreme Court ruled that all bus riders—regardless of race—could sit wherever they wanted.

From the 1880s through the 1960s, Jim Crow laws separated "colored," or black people, from white people in public places throughout the South.

In 1954 the U.S. Supreme Court ruled that it was illegal to have separate public schools for black students and white students. By 1963 African Americans had not been admitted to any state-run universities in Alabama. That year, a judge ordered the University of Alabama to allow two black students to enroll.

African Americans all over the country were treated unfairly in other ways as well. Although black men and women had the right to vote in the United States, many cities found ways to get around the law. These places required African Americans to pay a tax they couldn't afford or to take a test that many couldn't pass.

Governor George C. Wallace

George C. Wallace, born in Clio, Alabama, first became governor of the state in 1963, during the civil rights movement. That same year, Wallace showed the nation his position on civil rights by standing in the doorway to try and block two black students from entering the University of Alabama for the first time. But he could not change the law, and by the mid-1960s, many of Alabama's schools were attended by both black and white students.

Throughout his political career, Wallace insisted that he did not dislike black people but felt that both races would be better off if kept separate. His major complaint against civil rights laws was that they were set by the U.S. government. Wallace strongly believed in the right of each state to have control over its own affairs.

During the 1960s and 1970s, Wallace ran unsuccessfully for president of the United States. While campaigning in Maryland in 1972, he was shot five times. The incident left his legs paralyzed. He was elected to Alabama's governorship again in 1970, 1974, and 1982.

Wallace had always promised to help all needy Alabamians. During his last campaign for governor, his views on civil rights changed somewhat. He no longer wanted to keep blacks and whites separate and won the support of many black voters.

Protesters cross the Edmund Pettus Bridge on their way from Selma to Montgomery.

By 1965 the city of Selma, Alabama, still had not allowed most African American residents to register to vote. In protest, Martin Luther King, Jr., helped organize what started out as a peaceful march from Selma to Montgomery, the state capital.

Before they could even reach Montgomery, the protesters were stopped and beaten by state troopers. The day is remembered as Bloody Sunday. The marchers, however, did not give up. King scheduled another protest, leading 25,000 people to the steps of Montgomery's capitol building. Shortly afterward, the U.S. government outlawed the tough requirements used by southern states to keep black people from voting.

African Americans in Alabama began voting for politicians they felt would speak for them. Over the years, blacks have been elected to serve as mayors and city council members throughout the state.

6,000 B.C.   **A.D.1540**   **1702**   **1763**   **1814**   **1819**

People were living in what is now Alabama

Hernando de Soto attacks Choctaw Indians

The Le Moyne brothers establish Fort Louis de la Mobile

French and Indian War ends; Britain wins control over Alabama

Battle of Horseshoe Bend

Alabama becomes the 22nd state

Both black and white Alabamians, as well as other Americans, are still working to get along. Many Alabamians realize that the best future for their state is in providing the same opportunities to all its citizens.

To ensure that Alabamians have good jobs, Alabama has been working to attract new companies to the state. As a result, Alabama is now among the South's leading producers of high-tech products from medicine to rockets.

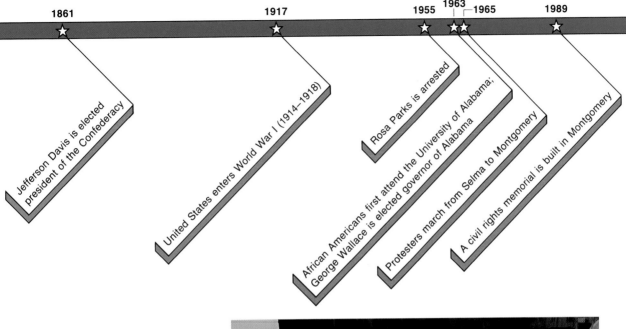

1861 — Jefferson Davis is elected president of the Confederacy

1917 — United States enters World War I (1914–1918)

1955 — Rosa Parks is arrested

1963 — African Americans first attend the University of Alabama; George Wallace is elected governor of Alabama

1965 — Protesters march from Selma to Montgomery

1989 — A civil rights memorial is built in Montgomery

...UNTIL JUSTICE ROLLS DOWN LIKE WATERS AND RIGHTEOUSNESS LIKE A MIGHTY STREAM

MARTIN LUTHER KING JR.

A memorial, built in 1989 outside the Southern Poverty Law Center in Montgomery, honors those who died in the civil rights movement.

A statue dedicated to the boll weevil has stood in downtown Enterprise since 1919.

Living and Working in Alabama

Enterprise, Alabama, may be the only city in the world with a statue honoring an insect. The town's citizens put up the monument to thank boll weevils for destroying most of the area's cotton crops in the early 1900s.

Why would a town do that? For many years, King Cotton determined how much money the people of Enterprise and other farming areas in Alabama made. When the cotton harvest was small or sold for low prices, everyone suffered. After the boll weevil invaded Alabama, farmers were forced to raise livestock and to plant crops that the beetle wouldn't attack. The farmers ended up making even more money than they had from cotton.

Dairy cattle wait to be milked. Most of the money made by Alabama's farmers comes from the sale of livestock products such as milk, eggs, and meat.

Alabama is still a leading cotton-growing state, but only $2 out of every $100 that farmers earn come from cotton. More than half of the money made from the state's farms is earned from livestock such as chickens, cattle, and hogs. Soybeans are the state's most valuable crop. Alabama's farmers also grow corn, hay, oats, wheat, pea-

Alabamians harvest cotton with machines called pickers. The machine pulls the cotton from the plant and then blows the fiber into a large metal basket.

Rocket Park, located outside the Marshall Space Flight Center, displays a lunar module. This spacecraft is used to land astronauts on the moon.

nuts, and pecans. Beekeepers raise bees for their honey and wax. Altogether, farmers make up 4 percent of the state's workforce.

Alabama's biggest moneymaker is services—that is, jobs where workers help other people or businesses. More than 1 million Alabamians—about 67 percent of the state's jobholders—are service workers. Among them are salespeople, doctors, social workers, bankers, teachers, and tour guides.

The U.S. and state governments employ about one in five of the service workers in Alabama. Soldiers stationed at military bases in the state fly jets, repair machinery, and direct air traffic. At the government-run George C. Marshall Space Flight Center, scientists design rockets.

45

Logs cut from Alabama's forests are stacked outside a mill.

Manufacturing employs 23 percent of Alabama's workforce. Laborers in the state's pulp and paper industry operate mills that process wood into paper, cardboard, and tissue. These products are treated with chemicals prepared in the state. Workers in the state's chemical plants also mix fertilizers and produce artificial fibers needed to make certain types of cloth.

Alabama ranks eighth in the nation in coal production. Thousands of the state's miners operate machines to dig for coal or to drill for oil and natural gas. Others scoop limestone out of the earth's surface for use in making steel and cement. Alabama's minerals and manufactured products are shipped to

Alabamians drill for oil in the Gulf of Mexico.

other states and countries from the Port of Mobile, one of the busiest ports in the nation.

The Port of Mobile handles about 40 million tons (36 million metric tons) of goods a year.

With a little more than 4 million people calling Alabama home, the 22nd state to join the Union ranks 22nd in the nation in population. About three out of every five Alabamians live in cities. The largest

A Native American plays a handmade flute at a festival in Moundville, Alabama.

of these are Birmingham, Mobile, Montgomery (the state capital), and Huntsville.

Most of Alabama's residents have English, French, or Spanish ancestors. One-fourth of the state's population is African American. Although several Indian nations once lived throughout the area, fewer than 8,000 Creek and Choctaw remain in Alabama.

Whatever their background, Alabamians have a rich history. Artifacts at the Indian Mound and Museum in Florence reveal the story of the state's mound-building Indians. At Fort Condé in Mobile, tour guides dressed in soldiers' uniforms tell stories about what life was like at the fort in the early 1700s. Visitors to Tuskegee can tour the George Washington Carver Museum. Exhibits there show the accomplishments of George Washington Carver, who studied plants and was one of the most famous instructors at Tuskegee Institute.

Paintings and sculptures draw crowds at the Birmingham Museum of Art. The Montgomery Museum of Fine Arts houses paintings

by southern artists and a special, hands-on gallery just for children. Music lovers can relax and enjoy symphony orchestras in Birmingham, Mobile, Huntsville, and Tuscaloosa. A stop in Florence will bring you to a childhood home of W. C. Handy, a musician known as the Father of the Blues.

Alabama is one of the few places in the country where folks can board a real battleship, the USS *Alabama*, anchored in Mobile Bay. Huntsville is home to the largest space museum in the world—the U.S. Space and Rocket Center.

USS *Alabama*

Visitors to the center can learn how it feels to walk in outer space, can examine rockets close-up, and can experience Journey to Jupiter—a combination ride and motion picture that makes you believe you've been to the planet. The U.S. Space Camp, which is part of the center, teaches young students about careers in aerospace.

Alabama offers a lot to sports enthusiasts. Hikers wander through giant caves at Carlsbad and Sequoyah caverns. Campers sleep under the stars in Conecuh, one of four national forests in Alabama. Boaters ride and fish in Alabama's lakes and in the Gulf of Mexico. Racing fans can watch Thoroughbred horses compete in Birmingham, greyhounds run in Tuskegee, or stock cars speed around the track at Talladega.

Each fall, people flock to the University of Alabama to cheer the

A young pilot operates a control panel at the U.S. Space Camp in Huntsville.

Crimson Tide, one of the best college football teams in the country. Excitement runs high when the Crimson Tide play their Alabama rival—the Tigers of Auburn University. The Birmingham Barons, a minor league baseball team, entertain Alabamians with one of America's best-loved sports.

Whether wanting to relax, to have fun, to glimpse at bygone days, or to peek into the future, people can find plenty to enjoy in Alabama—the Heart of Dixie.

Some government-owned forests have parks with scenic hiking trails.

Protecting the Environment

Forests cover more than two-thirds of Alabama and are one of the state's most important natural resources. The Port of Mobile exports about 2 million tons (1.8 million metric tons) of forest products, such as lumber and paper, every year. In addition to supplying timber, woodlands hold soil in place and provide homes for wildlife. Forests also serve as recreational areas and help make Alabama a beautiful place to live.

Some of Alabama's forests are run by the state or the U.S. government. These areas are meant to be enjoyed by all. Most of the state's forestland is owned and run by private individuals or companies. Much of Alabama's privately owned forestland is healthy, but some landowners unknowingly allow their forests' natural cycle of growth and decay to be disrupted.

Logs are taken from Alabama's forests by the truckload.

Some forest owners, for example, allow logging companies to cut down areas of forest without planning to create a new forest. While this practice gives new plants a chance to grow, creating homes for some animals, it also disturbs the habitat of other animals. And with no trees to hold soil in place, the soil may erode, or be washed away by rain.

To encourage landowners to take care of their forests, the Alabama Forestry Planning Committee de-

In a TREASURE Forest, seedlings *(below)* are planted to replace trees that have been cut down *(left).*

veloped the TREASURE Forest program in 1974. The letters in TREASURE stand for some important elements of a forest—Timber, Recreation, Environment, Aesthetics (or beauty), Sustained, Usable, and REsource. The program encourages private owners to get more than just timber out of their forestland.

Landowners who participate in this program decide on two or more main uses for their land. They can choose timber, wildlife, recreation, natural beauty, or environmental education. They also must agree to protect their forests from erosion, from water pollution, and from wildfires. Forests that meet the program's goals become TREASURE Forests.

TREASURE Forest landowners who manage their forests mainly for timber may need to thin out overcrowded stands of trees. When trees grow too close together, none of them grow very big. The larger the tree, the more money it will bring when sold for timber.

Black bears can be found in some wooded areas of Alabama.

Forest managers may even set fire to a small area of forest to encourage the growth of a particular tree, such as the longleaf pine. Longleaf pines, which are ideal for lumber and pulp, can survive fires that kill other trees. Once the other trees are burned, sunshine and bare soil allow longleaf pine seedlings to take root and thrive.

Managing a forest for timber also means growing new trees after harvesting to ensure a timber supply for the future. Nowadays, Alabama plants more trees than it harvests.

Burning undergrowth *(left)* **in a TREASURE Forest allows more light to reach the ground. Grass then carpets the forest floor** *(above),* **and cattle graze the pasture.**

59

Landowners who manage their forests for wildlife can increase the number and kinds of wild animals living there. Knowing that some animals need young forests and other animals need old forests, these landowners choose to raise a variety of trees in different stages of growth. These efforts have helped Alabama's animal population increase dramatically.

Nearly 1,000 Alabamians participate in the TREASURE Forest program. But that covers only about 7 percent of the state's forests. Some landowners don't join the program because they think the changes will cost too much and take too much effort.

Young people interested in forestry can get involved in the Junior TREASURE Forest program. Under this program, they thin stands of trees, plant new trees, and work on projects that help prevent soil erosion. Young and old people alike are working to make sure Alabama's forests have a healthy future.

TREASURE Forest owners strive to make the most of their forestland.

Alabama's Famous People

◄ HELEN KELLER

Helen Keller (1880–1968), from Tuscumbia, Alabama, lost her sight and hearing from an illness when she was 19 months old. With the help of her teacher, Ann Sullivan, Keller learned to speak and to read and write in Braille. Keller graduated with honors from Radcliffe College and devoted her life to improving conditions for the blind.

Coretta Scott King (born 1927), widow of civil rights leader Martin Luther King, Jr., works to promote the rights of minorities, women, and the unemployed. King was born near Marion, Alabama.

CORETTA SCOTT ►
KING

▼ JIM NABORS

ACTORS

Nell Carter (born 1948), a singer and actress, starred in the television series "Gimme A Break." In 1981 she won a Tony Award for her performance in the musical play *Ain't Misbehavin'.* Carter is originally from Birmingham.

Kate Jackson (born 1949) is an actress from Birmingham. She has played leading roles in several television series, including "Charlie's Angels" and "Scarecrow and Mrs. King." Jackson has also appeared in movies.

Jim Nabors (born 1932) played a goofy character named Gomer Pyle on "The Andy Griffith Show" and "Gomer Pyle, U.S.M.C."

▲ NELL
CARTER

KATE ►
JACKSON

He later hosted "The Jim Nabors Hour." Born in Sylacauga, Alabama, Nabors is also an established singer, having recorded five gold albums.

ATHLETES

HANK AARON

Hank Aaron (born 1934), a retired baseball player from Mobile, was one of the best home-run hitters of all time. Aaron spent most of his career with the Milwaukee (later Atlanta) Braves. 5 home runs, breaking Babe Ruth's all-

won four gold medals in track and field ames. He won medals in the 100-meter ash, the long jump, and the 400-meter irmingham.

CARL LEWIS ▶

), a native of Westfield, Alabama, was est athletes. Mays played center field San Francisco) Giants from 1951 until o the Baseball Hall of Fame in 1979.

AUTHORS

W. E. Butterworth (born 1929) is the author of more than 100 books, many of them for children. Because he writes so much, Butterworth was named the Most Prolific Alabama Author of All Time in 1971. His books, many of which he writes under different pen names, include *LeRoy and the Old Man* and *Susan and Her Classic Convertible.* Butterworth lives in Fairhope, Alabama.

Mark Childress (born 1957) is a writer from Monroeville, Alabama. His novels include *A World Made of Fire, V for Victor,* and *Crazy in Alabama.* Childress has also written *Joshua and Bigtooth,* a children's book.

Harper Lee (born 1926) won a Pulitzer Prize for her first and only novel, *To Kill a Mockingbird,* a young girl's account of her father defending a black man accused of a crime. The book has been translated into 10 languages. Lee is a native of Monroeville, Alabama.

◄ MARK CHILDRESS

◄ NAT KING COLE

EMMYLOU HARRIS ▼

◄ HANK WILLIAMS

MUSICIANS

Nat ("King") Cole (1917–1965) was a pianist and singer from Montgomery. His deep, mellow voice made him one of the most popular recording artists of the 1940s and 1950s. His many hits include "Straighten Up and Fly Right" and "Unforgettable."

Emmylou Harris (born 1947) is a country-music singer, songwriter, and guitarist. Her best-known albums include *Luxury Liner, Blue Kentucky Girl,* and *Cowgirl's Prayer.* She has won several Grammy Awards and in 1980 was voted Female Vocalist of the Year by the Country Music Association. Harris is originally from Birmingham.

Hank Williams (1923–1953) wrote and performed songs that made country music popular in regions other than the South and Southwest. A singer and guitarist from Georgiana, Alabama, Williams composed more than 100 tunes, including "Hey, Good Lookin'" and "Your Cheatin' Heart."

Hugo Black (1886–1971) was a U.S. senator from Alabama for 10 years before becoming a U.S. Supreme Court judge in 1937. Black, from Harlan, Alabama, strongly supported civil rights and free speech. He served on the court until his death.

Alexander McGillivray (1759?–1793), a leader of the Creek Indians, helped protect Creek land from white settlers by uniting the Creek and by signing treaties with the U.S. government. McGillivray was born near what is now Montgomery to a Scottish father and a half-French, half-Creek mother.

HUGO BLACK ▶

◀ GEORGE WASHINGTON CARVER

MAE JEMISON ▶

George Washington Carver (1864?–1943), a scientist and educator, went to Alabama in 1896 to teach agriculture at Tuskegee Institute (now Tuskegee University). One of the institute's most famous instructors and researchers, Carver developed more than 300 products from peanuts, including powdered milk and soap.

Mae C. Jemison (born 1956) is from Decatur, Alabama. In 1988 she became the first African American woman astronaut. In 1992 she was launched into orbit for the first time aboard the space shuttle *Endeavor*.

Facts-at-a-Glance

Nickname: Heart of Dixie
Song: "Alabama"
Motto: *Audemus Jura Nostra Defendere*
  (We Dare Defend Our Rights)
Flower: camellia
Tree: southern pine
Bird: yellowhammer

Population: 4,040,587*
Rank in population, nationwide: 22nd
Area: 52,423 sq mi (135,776 sq km)
Rank in area, nationwide: 30th
Date and ranking of statehood:
  December 14, 1819, the 22nd state
Capital: Montgomery
Major cities (and populations*):
  Birmingham (265,968), Mobile (196,278),
  Montgomery (187,106), Huntsville (159,789)
U.S. senators: 2
U.S. representatives: 7
Electoral votes: 9

Places to visit: Horseshoe Bend National Military Park in Tallapoosa County, U.S. Space and Rocket Center in Huntsville, Bellingrath Gardens and Home in Theodore, First White House of the Confederacy in Montgomery, Russell Cave National Monument near Bridgeport

Annual events: Mardi Gras in Mobile (Feb.), Southeastern Livestock Exposition Rodeo and Livestock Week in Montgomery (March–April), Alabama June Jam Week in Fort Payne (June), Arlington Country Fair in Birmingham (Sept.), Holiday Festival in Selma (Dec.)

*1990 census

Natural resources: forests, soil, rivers, coal, limestone, oil, natural gas

Agricultural products: milk, eggs, chickens, beef cattle, hogs, soybeans, cotton, corn, hay, oats, wheat, peanuts, pecans

Manufactured goods: paper products, clothing, chemicals, steel, cement, food products

ENDANGERED SPECIES
Mammals—gray bat, Alabama beach mouse
Birds—American peregrine falcon, bald eagle, wood stork, Eskimo curlew, red-cockaded woodpecker
Reptiles—leatherback sea turtle, Alabama red-bellied turtle
Fish—spring pygmy sunfish, watercress darter, boulder darter, cahaba shiner, Alabama cavefish
Plants—Alabama leather flower, leafy prairie-clover, pondberry, harperella

WHERE ALABAMIANS WORK
Services—48 percent
  (services includes jobs in trade; community, social, & personal services; finance, insurance, & real estate; transportation, communication, & utilities)
Manufacturing—23 percent
Government—19 percent
Construction—5 percent
Agriculture—4 percent
Mining—1 percent

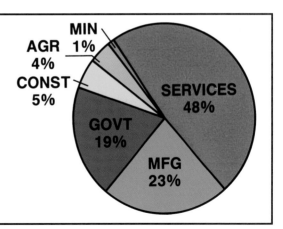

AGR 4%
MIN 1%
CONST 5%
SERVICES 48%
GOVT 19%
MFG 23%

PRONUNCIATION GUIDE

Chattahoochee (chat-uh-HOO-chee)

Cheaha (CHEE-haw)

Cherokee (CHEHR-uh-kee)

Chickasaw (CHIHK-uh-saw)

Choctaw (CHAHK-taw)

Dauphin (DAW-fuhn)

Le Moyne, Pierre and Jean Baptiste
  (luh mwahn, pee-YEHR and
  zhawn bah-TEEST)

Muskogean (muhs-KOH-gee-uhn)

Sequoyah (sih-KWOY-uh)

Tecumseh (tuh-KUHMP-suh)

Tombigbee (tahm-BIHG-bee)

Tuskegee (tuhs-KEE-gee)

Glossary

carpetbagger   A term used by Southerners to describe Northerners who came to the South after the Civil War to make money. The name carpetbagger suggests that Northerners carried everything they owned in a carpetbag, or suitcase.

civil rights movement   A movement to gain equal rights, or freedoms, for all citizens—regardless of race, religion, sex.

colony   A territory ruled by a country some distance away.

lock   An enclosed water-filled chamber in a canal or river used to raise or lower boats beyond the site of a waterfall. Boats can enter the lock through a gate at either end.

plantation   A large estate, usually in a warm climate, on which crops are grown by workers who live on the estate. In the past, plantation owners usually used slave labor.

precipitation   Rain, snow, and other forms of moisture that fall to earth.

Reconstruction   The period from 1865 to 1877 during which the U.S. government brought the Southern states back into the Union after the Civil War. Before rejoining the Union, a Southern state had to pass a law allowing black men to vote. Places destroyed in the war were rebuilt and industries were developed.

reservoir   A place where water is collected and stored for later use.

swamp   A wetland permanently soaked with water. Woody plants (trees and shrubs) are the main form of vegetation.

Index

Acknowledgments:

Maryland Cartographics, Inc., pp. 2, 11; William H. Allen, Jr., pp. 2–3, 12, 13, 17 (top left), 19 (top), 43, 44, 48, 49; NE Stock Photo: Jim Schwabel, pp. 6, 41, 54, Jean Higgins, pp. 16, 50–51, Robert Boyer, pp. 46, 55, Bill Lea, p. 57; Jack Lindstrom, p. 7; Johnny Autery, pp. 8–9, 10, 14; Jerry Hennen, pp. 15, 17 (inset); Lynn M. Stone, p. 17 (bottom left); Root Resources: Mary A. Root, pp. 17 (right), 42, Paul C. Hodge, p. 68; Tennessee State Museum, from a painting by Carlyle Urello, p. 20 (inset); Library of Congress, pp. 20, 23, 26–27, 29, 31, 65 (top); Museums of the City of Mobile, pp. 21, 24; IPS, p. 22; Smithsonian Institution, p. 28; AmSouth Bank, p. 30; University of South Alabama Archives: Erik Overbey Collection, p. 32, Addsco Collection, p. 35; Minneapolis Public Library, p. 33; Schomberg Center for Research in Black Culture, the New York Public Library, Astor, Lenox, and Tilden, p. 36; Archives Collection, Birmingham Public Library, Birmingham, AL, p. 37; Alabama Dept. of Archives and History, p. 38; UPI / Bettmann, p. 39; Frederica Georgia, p. 45; Barbara Laatsch-Hupp / Laatsch-Hupp Photo, p. 47; Bob Gathany / U.S. Space and Rocket Center, p. 52; Alabama Bureau of Tourism and Travel, p. 53; © James A. Deason II, pp. 56 (both), 70; Alabama Forestry Commission, pp. 58–59 (both), 61 (both); *Dictionary of American Portraits*, p. 62 (top left); Boston University Photo Service, p. 62 (top right); Hollywood Book & Poster Co., pp. 62 (center left, center right, bottom), 64 (bottom); Atlanta Braves, p. 63 (top left); University of Houston, p. 63 (top right); San Francisco Giants, p. 63 (bottom); Jerry Bauer / G. P. Putnam's Sons, p. 64 (top); TV Times, p. 64 (center left); Caroline Greyshock, p. 64 (center right); USDA, p. 65 (bottom left); NASA, p. 65 (bottom right); Jean Matheny, p. 66.